BAKED RACOON
(Odawa)

1 racoon, cleaned with fat removed and
   cut up in pieces
Tomato juice
Onions, diced
Carrots, diced
Potatoes, diced
Salt and pepper tc

CW01502351

Put raccoon meat in a large pot and cover with water.
Bring to a boil then simmer until meat is tender.
Remove meat from a pot and place in a baking dish.
Add onions, carrots and tomatoes to the dish and salt
and pepper to taste. Pour tomato juice over all of the
ingredients. Cover the dish and bake at 350 degrees for
1 hour or until the vegetables are cooked.

BANAHA a.k.a. CORN SHUCK BREAD
(Choctaw)

2 cups of cornmeal
1 teaspoon of baking soda
1½ cups of hot water
1 teaspoon of salt
Corn shucks (boil 10 minutes before using)

Mix the cornmeal, baking soda and salt together thoroughly. Add water until mixture is stiff and easy to handle. Form the batter into small oblong balls and wrap in corn shucks. Tie the shucks in the middle with corn shuck string. Drop the covered balls into a deep pot of boiling water. Cover and cook 40 minutes. Remove the shucks before serving.

BANNOCK
(Blackfoot)

6 cups of white flour
2½ cups of water
3 tablespoons of baking powder
1½ teaspoons of salt

In a bowl mix flour, baking powder and salt together thoroughly. Stir in water to the mixture slowly until thick dough forms. Place the dough on a lightly floured surface. Flatten out the dough and form it into a lightly greased 9-inch by 13-inch baking dish or pan. Bake at 350 degrees for 35 minutes. It should turn a light brown when done. Turn on to a board or rack and slice into 6 pieces while warm.

BEAN BREAD
(Cherokee)

2 cups of milk
1 cup of cornmeal
1 cup of flour
1 cup of shortening, melted
1 egg, beaten
2 tablespoons of honey
1 tablespoon of sugar
2 teaspoons of baking powder
4 cups of brown beans, drained

Mix all ingredients together thoroughly except the beans. After the batter is consistent, fold in the beans slowly. Pour the batter into a greased warm baking dish or pan. Bake at 450 degrees for 30 minutes until brown.

BEAR CHOPS
(Tlingit)

6 medium bear chops
1 clove of garlic, halved
2 tablespoons of bacon fat
1 large onion, diced
4 large carrots, diced and cooked
4 tablespoons of unbleached all-purpose flour
4 tablespoons of chili sauce
½ cup of dry wine
Salt and pepper to taste

Rub the chops with the halved garlic cloves. Melt the bacon fat in a cast iron skillet and sear the chops on both sides. Place the chops in a lightly greased baking dish. Sauté the onions and carrots in the skillet until the onions are transparent but not brown. Mix in the flour, chili sauce and wine. Cook until thickened. On top of each chop, place an equal amount of the carrot mixture. Pour 1 cup of water into the baking dish; cover with foil and bake at 375 degrees for 60 to 70 minutes or until tender.

BEAVER BALL SOUP
(Metis)

10-20 beaver balls
1 cup of macaroni
1 jar of stewed tomatoes
Salt and pepper to taste

In a pot, boil the beaver balls. Stir in the macaroni and tomatoes. Salt and pepper the mixture to taste. Let simmer for 1 hour. If beaver balls are not to your liking or are difficult to find there are alternatives. Make meatballs out of ground moose, deer, elk or bear meat.

BERRY SOUP
(Ojibwe)

4 cups of Saskatoon or blueberries
4 cups of rhubarb, chopped
4 apples, diced
½ cup of raisins
Water

Clean and wash the fruit and rhubarb. In a pot combine berries, rhubarb, apples and raisins. Cover with enough water to simmer. Bring to a boil then simmer for 30 minutes. Cool and serve.

BLUE BREAD
(Navajo)

1 cup of juniper ash
1 cup of boiling water
2 cups of water
3½ cups of boiling water
6 cups of blue cornmeal
½ teaspoon of salt
Oil

Mix the juniper ash with 1 cup of boiling water. Put 3½ cups of water in a pot and boil. Strain the juniper water into a pot. Add 6 cups of blue cornmeal. Knead the dough until it's soft but firm. Shape into 24 small patties. Put on a lightly oiled hot skillet. Cook until brown on each side. Mix salt with 2 cups of water. Dip the bread into the salt water.

BLUE CAMAS BULBS
(Nez Perce)

½ pound of blue camas bulbs
1 tablespoon of olive oil, butter or fat
1 tablespoon of lemon juice or
   white wine vinegar
Smoked salt
Fine salt

Remove the papery sheath from the bulbs and place in baking dish with a lid. Pour in just enough water to cover the bottom of the container with a ¼-inch. Cover the container and bake the camas bulbs at 225 degrees for 12 hours. Check after 8 hours or so. You want them to range from pale gold to full gold. Slice the bulbs into rings and lightly dust them with fine salt. Sauté them in olive oil, butter or fat until they are brown. Keep stirring to prevent them from sticking. When done, toss with lemon juice or white wine vinegar and dust with the smoked salt.

BOILED MOOSE RIBS
(Yupik)

10 moose ribs
Seal oil
Salt
Water

Cut the ribs off the moose. Put them in a pot. Set the stove on medium heat and cook for 1 hour. Cool and eat with seal oil and salt.

BUFFALO & RICE SOUP
(Winnebago)

3 pounds of ground buffalo
5 cups of water
2 cups of rice (white, brown or wild)
1 teaspoon of beef base

In a pot, boil the water. Add beef base and rice to the boiling water and cover the pot. While rice is cooking, brown the buffalo meat in a skillet. Drain the meat of the liquid and add to the boiling water. Cook until rice splits. Season to taste.

BUTTER FRIED MOREL MUSHROOMS
(Odawa)

20 fresh-picked morel mushrooms
½ cup of flour
1 stick of flour
1 tablespoon of oil
Salt and pepper to taste

Cut the mushrooms in half. Wash in salted water and remove any bugs or foreign matter hiding in the creases. Drain well. Mix flour, salt and pepper in a Ziploc bag. Drop morels in the bag and shake to coat thoroughly. Heat butter and oil in a skillet slowly. Do not let it burn. Add a few morels at a time, frying 2 to 3 minutes per side.

CARIBOU SOUP
(Inuit)

1 pound of caribou meat, cut into small pieces
2 celery stalks, diced
1 onion, diced
1 carrot, diced
1 cup of macaroni
1 cup of rice
4 tablespoons of oil
Garlic or onion salt to taste
Salt and pepper to taste
2½ quarts of water

Sauté caribou meat in a pot with the oil. Add salt, garlic salt and onion salt to taste. Pepper is optional. Add in onion, carrots and celery and sauté in oil with the meat. Cover meat and vegetables with the water. Cover the pot and cook for 30 minutes. Add potatoes, rice and macaroni and cook on low for another 30 minutes. Stir to prevent sticking.

CHAPARRAL TEA
(Coquille)

Dried wild lilac leaves
Hot water

Pick and dry these leaves. They leaves are not commercially sold. Steep one teaspoon of dry leaves per cup of hot water. Adjust to taste.

CHERRY SAUCE
(Mandan)

2 cups of water
2 cups of dried cherries, add water to plump
¼ cup of all-purpose flour
2 tablespoons of honey
1/8 teaspoon of salt

In a pan, combine 2 cups of water, ¼ cup of flour, 2 tablespoons of honey and salt. Mix the ingredients thoroughly. Stir in the plumbed dried cherries and bring the mixture to a boil. Reduce heat to low. Cook and continue to stir until the mixture thickens and bubbles. Serve hot.

CHINOOK NUT CORNBREAD
(Chinook)

1 cup of cornmeal
1 cup of creamed corn
½ cup of flour
½ cup of milk
¼ - ½ cup of almonds
2 eggs
Yeast

In a bowl mix flour, creamed corn, cornmeal and yeast thoroughly. Stir in eggs, almonds and milk to the mixture. Pour batter into a lightly greased loaf pan or baking dish. Bake at 350 degrees for 30 minutes or until golden brown.

COOPEE`
(Blackfoot)

1 cup of dried Sarvis, June or Service berries
4 cups of water
½ cup of flour
Sugar to taste

In a pot boil berries in the water until soft. Slowly stir in the flour until the soup begins to thicken. Add sugar to taste.

CORN BREAD
(Oneida)

2 cups of white corn flour
1¾ cups of boiling water
½ cup of cooked beans (kidney, red or pinto)
¼ teaspoon of salt

Combine flour, salt and beans. Add the boiling water and mix thoroughly. Dip hands in cold water before working the very hot dough. Shape the dough into a ball then flatten to a 4-inch circle. In a large pot, boil the dough for 30 minutes.

CORN CHOWDER
(Navajo)

4 slices of pork, diced
½ cup of wild onions, diced
2 cups of fresh corn kernels
4 tablespoons of wheat flour
1 cup of arrowhead tubers, peeled
2½ cups of chicken broth
½ cup of cold water
1 pint of hot milk

Fry the salt pork slowly in a deep frying pan until it's crisp. Add onions and cook until they turn a golden brown. Stir in the tubers and the chicken broth. Cover and simmer for 20 minutes. Add the fresh corn and simmer for 15 minutes. Mix the flour with water and stir until it becomes a smooth paste. Add to the frying pan and bring to a boil. Stir constantly. Stir in the milk and reheat without boiling. Season to taste.

CORN STEW
(Hopi)

2 cups of green corn, cut from the cob
1 cup of summer squash, cubed
1 cup of goat meat, ground
1 sweet green pepper, diced
1 tablespoon of whole-wheat flour
Salt to taste
Oil
Water

In a pot, brown the meat in a little bit of oil. Add pepper, corn and squash and cover with water. Simmer until the vegetables are almost tender, 8 to 12 minutes. Combine the flour with 2 tablespoons of water to make a paste and stir into the pot. Simmer for 5 minutes and keep stirring.

CORN WASNA
(Dakota)

2 cups of yellow cornmeal
1 cup of raisins
1½ cups of sugar
1 cup + 5 tablespoons of hot tallow with
  cracklings
1½ cups of nonfat dry milk
1 teaspoon of salt

In a baking dish, heat the cornmeal in a baking dish at
325 degrees until the cornmeal is very brown. Mix the
cornmeal, sugar, fruit and salt together thoroughly.
Add the tallow and mix well. Press into an 8-inch by
8-inch pan and allow to cool.

DRIED MOOSE MEAT
(Yupik)

Raw moose meat
Bowl of sauce

Cut the moose meat in strips and marinate in your sauce of choice for 30 minutes. Hang the meat outside on a long horizontal pole until dry.

EEL AKUTAQ a.k.a. EEL ICE CREAM
(Yupik)

Eels
Berries
Lard
Water

In a pot, boil eels for 2½ hours. Wring excess water and fat from the eels. Mix with lard thoroughly then mix berries of choice to your taste.

ELIXIR REMEDY
(Kickapoo)

Fifth of white whiskey
 (non-barrel aged, legal "moonshine"
20 ounces of strawberries
2¼ cups of brown sugar
3 cups of tea made from American ginseng
 root or ginger root, cloves and peppercorns

Clean, wash and slice the strawberries. Soak the berries in the whiskey for 2 days. Boil spring water. Dissolve brown sugar in 3 cups of the hot water. Pour the hot sugar water over ginseng or ginger root, cloves and peppercorns. Cover the tea and let cool. Remove the strawberries from the whiskey. Mix tea and whiskey and drink as a restorative.

FISH AND CATTAILS
(Cheyenne)

2 quarts of cattail shoots or young stems,
    washed
4 bass or trout fillets
2 cups of water
Salt to taste
Crushed red pepper, to taste

Harvest spring cattail shoots or green, new stems. Put
fish fillets in a skillet and lay cattails on tops. Pour
water into the skillet and cover. Steam for 5 to 10
minutes. Season with salt and crushed red pepper.

FISH HEAD STEW
(Yurok)

1 salmon head
1 skein of salmon row
½ piece of salmon backbone
5 chunks of salmon
1 salmon tail
4 potatoes, peeled and diced
2 cups of celery, diced
1 onion, diced
1 can of corn
Salt and pepper to taste
Water

Put salmon head, salmon row, celery, onion, potato, salmon chunks, salmon backbone, corn and salmon tail in a stew pot. Add in enough water to cover 2 inches above the ingredients. Boil until potatoes and fish are done. Salt and pepper to taste. Watch out for small bones.

FISH WITH DANDELIONS
(Cree)

2 trout, salmon or bass
6 handfuls of dandelion greens
3 wild onions
2 pinches of white sage
1 lemon
Bacon grease
Salt and pepper to taste

Cut and clean the fish. Then cut the fish into long strips. Dice the onion and thinly slice the lemon. Wash and chop the dandelion leaves. Grease a skillet with bacon grease and put on medium heat. Add fish strips, onion, 6 thin slices of lemon, salt, pepper and white sage to the skillet. Cook until ingredients are 75% done then add the dandelion leaves. Cook until leaves are soft. Add salt, pepper and white sage again. Just before serving drizzle with lemon juice. If ingredients stick to the skillet, add in a little more bacon grease. The fish should brown just a bit.

FRIED SEAL LIVER
(Aleut)

Seal liver, in bite-size pieces
Flour
Onion, diced
Soy sauce
Oil or fat

Dredge the pieces of liver in flour. In a skillet, fry in hot oil or fat. Stir in onions while cooking. Sprinkle with soy sauce or keep it on the side for dipping.

FRIED YUCCA PETALS
(Cherokee)

1 flower stalk from a yucca plant
1 cup of water
2 fresh tomatoes, diced
2 onions, diced
1 tablespoon of shortening
Salt and pepper to taste

Pull flower petals from stalk and wash in salt water. Melt the shortening in a skillet and add petals, onion and tomatoes. Stir gently until the onions are soft. Add water and simmer until most of the liquid is gone. Salt and pepper to taste.

FRY BREAD
(Apache)

2½ cups of flour
1 cup of water
1 teaspoon of baking powder
1 teaspoon of salt
Fat or oil

Mix the first four ingredients thoroughly and knead until uniform. Roll the dough to ½-inch thick and cut into squares. In a deep skillet, fry the pieces in at least 2 inches of fat or oil. Flip the pieces until browned on both sides.

GHOST BREAD
(Seneca)

2 cups of flour
1 cup of warm water
¼ cup of dry milk
¼ cup of shortening or lard
2 teaspoons of baking powder
1/8 teaspoon of salt

In a bowl combine all ingredients except shortening or lard. Mix thoroughly until batter is smooth. In a skillet heat shortening or lard with medium heat until it melts. With a wooden spoon scoop a large dollop of the full batter and place it in the shortening. Fry for 30 seconds or until bottom is firm enough to slip spatula under and flip. Carefully turn the dough over and press flat with a spatula. You might have to press it down a few times. When it gets light brown around the edges turn it over and cook until edges are browned.

GRILLED PRAIRIE DOG
(Navajo)

5 fresh prairie dogs
Onions
Garlic
Salt
Pepper

Clean and quarter prairie dogs. Pat the meat dry. Put the meat on a griddle or in a skillet on a grill or stove. Add in onions, garlic, salt and pepper to taste. Grill slowly for 30 to 35 minutes.

HIDATSA PUMPKIN
(Hidatsa)

1 five-pound sugar pumpkin
2 teaspoons of salt
½ teaspoon of dry mustard
2 tablespoons of vegetable oil or rendered fat
1 pound of ground, venison, buffalo or beef
1 medium onion, diced
1 cup of wild or brown rice, cooked
3 eggs, beaten
1 teaspoon of crushed dried sage
¼ teaspoon of pepper

Cut the top off of the pumpkin, like you would for a Jack O'Lantern. Remove the seeds and strings from the pumpkin. Prick the cavity with a fork all over and rub with 1 teaspoon of salt and the dry mustard throughout. Heat oil in large skillet. Add meat and onion and sauté over medium-high heat until browned. Remove from the heat and stir in wild rice, eggs, remaining salt, sage and pepper. Stuff the pumpkin with this mixture. Place ½-inch of water in the bottom of a shallow baking pan and place the pumpkin with the lid on, in the pan and bake for 90 minutes or until tender. Add more water to the pan as necessary to avoid sticking.

HUCKLEBERRY BREAD
(Cherokee)

2 cups of flour, self-rising
2 cups of huckleberries
1 cup of sugar
1 cup of milk
1 egg
1 stick of butter
1 teaspoon of vanilla extract

Cream the egg, butter and sugar together thoroughly. Stir in the flour, milk and vanilla to the cream mixture. Save a little flour to sprinkle on the berries to prevent them from sinking to the bottom of the batter. Stir the berries into the batter. Pour into a lightly greased baking pan and bake at 350 degrees for 35 to 40 minutes.

HULL CORN SOUP
(Oneida)

2 cups of dehydrated corn
12 ounces of salt pork or venison, cooked
2 cups of beans, cooked
   (red, kidney, or pinto beans)
12 ounces of salt pork or venison, cooked

Soak the corn over night in enough water to cover the kernels. Drain. Add enough water to cover the corn about 1 inch then bring to a boil. Cover and simmer for 1 hour. Add the beans and cooked salt pork or venison to the pot. Simmer 1-2 hours. Add more water to cover the ingredients throughout the cooking process.

.

HUZUSUKI a.k.a FINGER BREAD
(Hopi)

1¾ cup of blue corn meal,
 ground medium fine
2 cups of water

In a pot, bring water to a boil then reduce the heat to low. Slowly add in the cornmeal, stirring constantly. A stiff dough will form. Spoon the cooked dough on to a plate.

MILKWEED SOUP
(Ho Chunk)

Top leaves of the milkweed
Blossoms of the milkweed
Salt
Pot of water

Gather the top 4 leaves of the plant in early spring.
Pick the little blossoms too. The pot should be half
leaves and blossom and half water. Soak the leaves
and blossoms for 1 hour in the pot of water. Add a
pinch or two of salt. Bring the pot of water to a boil.
Boil for 30 to 40 minutes. Stir occasionally.

MOOSE MEAT CHILI
(Maliseet)

2 pounds of moose meat, ground
2 cloves of garlic, minced
2 onions, diced
4 cups of water
2 cups of tomato sauce
4 tablespoons of chili powder
1 tablespoon of unsweetened cocoa
1 tablespoon of vinegar
1 teaspoon of cumin
1 teaspoon of paprika
1 teaspoon of salt
1 teaspoon of honey or molasses
½ teaspoon of pepper
½ teaspoon of all spice
½ teaspoon of cinnamon
1 can of dark red kidney beans
1 can of black bean

In a large pot, boil moose meat in 4 cups of water for 30 minutes. Stir in remaining ingredients except the beans. Simmer the mixture for 3 hours uncovered. Add beans and simmer for 1 more hour.

MOOSE MEAT SOUP
(Yupik)

1 pound of moose meat
½ gallon of water
1 cup of rice
1 cup of macaroni
¼ cup of salt
¼ cup of dried onions

Cut and clean the moose meat. Put the moose meat, onions and salt in a pot with the water. When the pot starts to boil, turn the heat down and let it boil for 45 minutes. Add rice and macaroni to the pot and boil for 15 to 20 minutes. Then the soup will be done.

PAN FRIED BANNOCK
(Inuit)

2 cups of flour
2 cups of water
1 cup of raisins
3 tablespoons of baking powder
1 tablespoon of lard
2 eggs (optional)
½ cup of sugar (optional)

Put the flour in a bowl and add baking powder. Stir it thoroughly. Add raisins and water and mix well. Put 1 tablespoon of lard into a skillet and melt it. Pour the bannock into pan and cook it. Rotate the bannock so it cooks evenly, check with a fork to see if it's cooked inside. Cook on both sides.

PEMMICAN
(Crow)

Dry meat
Chokecherries, ground
Lard or tallow
Sugar

In a large pan mix the dry meat with equal parts chokecherries and sugar. Melt lard until soft but not turning to liquid. Pour lard into the pan and stir until a ball forms. Put the pemmican in the refrigerator until ready to serve.

PINON CAKES
(Cherokee)

3 cups of pinon (pine) nuts
1 cup + 2 tablespoons of water
3 tablespoons of salt
½ teaspoon of salt

Puree the nuts or chop them into a consistency of a course meal. Blend with salt and water and let the batter rest for 1 hour. Heat the oil in a skillet. Form the batter into 8 to 10 3-inch cakes. Brown cakes on both sides.

ROAST GOOSE
(Yupik)

   1 goose
   6 potatoes, cut-up
   1 onion, sliced
   1 tablespoon of seasoning

Cut of the goose into 4 or more parts. Wash the meat in clean water. Put a little bit of water in a pot. Put the goose parts in the pot and boil for 20 to 25 minutes. Add potatoes, onions and seasonings. Place the goose in the oven and broil at 350 degrees for 1 hour.

SASSAFRASS CHERRY TEA
(Shawnee)

3 cups of sassafras roots, grated
2 quarts of water
2 cups of wild cherries, crushed
1 cup of honey

Put water, sassafras and wild cherries in a pot. Boil for 10 minutes. Take off the heat and strain the tea. Add honey and drink.

SEA LION SOUP
(Aleut)

1 pound of sea lion meat, cubed
6 cups of water
4 stalks of celery with tops
1 onion, diced
1 potato diced
½ cup of rice, uncooked
1 teaspoon of Worcestershire sauce
2 tablespoons of flour
2 tablespoons of water
Wild parsley
Salt and pepper to taste

Boil sea lion meat in 6 cups of water for 45 minutes. Stir in celery, parsley, potato, rice, onion, salt and pepper. Make a paste of the flour and 2 tablespoons of water. Add more water if needed. Stir into soup until meat is tender and soup thickens.

PERSIMMON CAKE
(Choctaw)

1 cup of persimmon cake
1 cup of flour
½ cup of sugar
1 egg, slightly beaten
2 tablespoons of butter, softened
1 teaspoon of baking powder
½ teaspoon of baking soda

In a bowl mix all ingredients thoroughly. Pour the batter into a greased and floured baking pan. Bake at 350 degrees for 40 minutes.

SALMON ON A STICK
(Grand Ronde)

Salmon or any available fish

Build a fire. Clean the fish and cut it in half or into meal-size chunks. Skewer the fish on a stick. Place the fish on a stick into the ground close to the hot coals. Turn the fish, as the bottom will cook quickly. Don't underestimate the speed at which the fish will cook on the stick. Season as you like.

SOFKEE
(Seminole)

2 quarts of water (salted if you prefer)
2 cups of wild rice
3 tablespoons of cornstarch
1 teaspoon of baking soda

In a large pot, bring the water to a boil. Add the rice and cornstarch to the water. Stir occasionally to prevent the rice from sticking to the bottom. Boil for 10 to 12 minutes. Reduce the heat and stir in the baking soda. Keep stirring until the rice is tender.

SPICEWOOD TEA
(Cherokee)

Spicewood Twigs
Water
Molasses or honey

Place water and twigs in a pot and boil. Serve the drink hot. Sweeten with molasses or honey. The more twigs you use the stronger the tea.

TANICA
(Passamaquoddy)

Tripe
Potatoes (equal to ½ of the amount of tripe)
Onion to taste, diced

Clean the tripe well and cut into bite-sized pieces.
Boil the tripe for 4 hours but don't let it get mushy.
Peel and dice the potatoes and slice the onion into
rings. Add potato and onion during the last 30 minutes
of cooking.

THREE SISTERS SOUP
(Iroquois)

5 cups of water

2 cups of canned white or yellow hominy,
   drained

2 cups of fresh green beans,
   trimmed and snapped

2 cups of butternut squash, peeled and cubed

1½ cups of potatoes, peeled and diced

1½ tablespoons of chicken bouillon granules

2 tablespoons of butter, melted

2 tablespoons of all-purpose flour

¼ teaspoon of pepper

Place the hominy, green beans, squash and potatoes into a pot. Pour water and chicken bouillon into the pot. Stir the mixture thoroughly. Bring the mixture to a boil and then reduce heat to low. Simmer for 10 minutes or until vegetables are soft. Blend the flour with the butter to make a paste then stir into the soup. Increase heat to medium and cook for 5 minutes or until the soup thickens. Season the soup with pepper.

TISWIN
(Pueblo)

5 pounds of dried white corn
2 gallons of water
1½ cups of brown sugar
3 cinnamon sticks
2 dried orange peels
1 teaspoon of ground cloves

Roast the corn in the oven, stirring frequently, until it turns light brown. Grind the corn coarsely in a food chopper, blender or food processor. Wash and rinse the corn a few times, discarding the hulls. Put the corn into a crock and stir in water and remaining ingredients. Cover and let rest for 5 to 6 days or until fermented. Strain through cheesecloth and serve.

TORTILLAS
(Ute)

3 cups of unbleached flour
2 teaspoons of baking powder
   (3 teaspoons at high altitudes)
1 teaspoon of salt
1½ cups of warm water or milk
1 tablespoon of oil or shortening

Combine all of the ingredients except the oil and knead until smooth. Rub oil all over the dough and cover. Let this dough rest for 30 minutes. Divide the dough into 10 equal parts and roll out into a circular shape one-eighth inch thick and 6 inches in diameter. Cook the dough on a charcoal grill or over an open fire.

WAMPANACKALI
(Wyandot)

9 cups of venison (shredded, diced, etc.)
2 cups of squirrel (shredded, diced, etc)
1 teaspoon of honey
¼ teaspoon of lemon juice
Salt and pepper to taste

In a large pot or baking dish mix venison, squirrel, honey, salt and pepper. Cook or bake until the meat is tender. Sprinkle lemon juice on the mixture just before serving.

WHITE CEDAR TEA
(Mohawk)

2 large handfuls of white cedar needles
1 teapot full of water
Honey
Lemon juice, fresh squeezed

Put the needles into the water and boil until the water turns a rich green color. Remove from heat and strain out the needles. Pour a cup of the tea and add a teaspoon of honey and lemon to taste.

WILD PEPPERMINT TEA
(Sioux)

½ cup of dry peppermint leaves
3-4 cups of water
2-3 tablespoons of honey

Bring water to a boil. Add peppermint leaves and shut off heat. Let tea steep for 5 minutes then pour through a strainer. Add honey and serve.

WOODCHUCK STEW
(Mohawk)

1 woodchuck (a.k.a. ground hog),
  cleaned and filleted
2 quarts of water
3 potatoes
2 carrots
2 cloves of garlic
1 onion
1 red pepper
1 green pepper
1 handful of pigweed

Cut meat into 1-inch chunks. Put into a large pot with water. Add ingredients and salt and pepper to taste. Boil until it's cooked.

For more information on
"Flannel John's Cookbooks for Guys" and
Tim Murphy's other books visit
www.flanneljohn.com.

Printed in Great Britain
by Amazon